UNIVERSITY OF MINNESOTA

PAMPHLETS ON AMERICAN WRITERS • NUMBER 42

American Humorists

BY WI

UNIVERSITY OF MINNESOTA PRESS • MINNEAPOLIS

Printed in the United States of America at
the North Central Publishing Company, St. Paul

Library of Congress Catalog Card Number: 64-64449

Distributed to high schools in the United States by Webster Division
McGraw-Hill Book Company, Inc.
St. Louis New York San Francisco Dallas

PUBLISHED IN GREAT BRITAIN, INDIA, AND PAKISTAN BY THE OXFORD UNIVERSITY PRESS, LONDON, BOMBAY, AND KARACHI, AND IN CANADA BY THE COPP CLARK PUBLISHING CO. LIMITED, TORONTO

AMERICAN HUMORISTS

WILLARD THORP, an adviser for the series of University of Minnesota Pamphlets on American Writers, is the Holmes Professor of Belles Lettres at Princeton University.

American Humorists

AMERICANS, in the early days, imported much of their humor and made it over. Addison and Steele were influential; Dickens had his American imitators. Baron Munchausen's adventures were particularly popular in this country. Many of his tales disappeared into American folklore and rose again as transformed American tall tales.

By the 1830's it was apparent that a brand of native humor was developing on these shores which was distinctive in subject, character, setting, and manner of telling. European travelers took note of the fact. Captain Frederick Marryat's *A Diary in America* (1839) has a perceptive chapter on "Language" in which he gives some samples of the energetic metaphors in the new American idiom. "I wish I had all hell boiled down to a point," one gentleman remarked to him, "just to pour down your throat."

Though no American writers in the seventeenth and eighteenth centuries devoted themselves to humor exclusively, the chroniclers described the incongruities of colonial life and drew humor from the regional types they encountered. When Sarah Kemble Knight made the rugged journey from Boston to New York in 1704, her tribulations were lightened by the odd folk she met along the way and she recorded their speech and manners in her journal. The Virginian William Byrd also had an eye for the ridiculous. As one of the commissioners who in 1728 surveyed the line between Virginia and North Carolina, he kept a "Secret History" of the trip which he later enlarged as *History of the Dividing Line*. Its devastating description of the North Carolina poor whites is funny to all readers except Carolinians.

Benjamin Franklin used humor to entertain and covertly to instruct in the Silence Dogood letters he contributed anonymously in 1722 to his brother's *New England Courant.* Ten years later he issued his first *Poor Richard's Almanack,* for the year 1733. The famous character there created was enlarged upon year by year as Franklin re-introduced him annually from 1733 to 1758. Richard's sayings are drawn from a great variety of sources, but Franklin pointed up what he appropriated. Thus the proverb "Fresh fish and new come guests smell by they are three days old" became "Fish and visitors stink in three days."

Humor and satire were two weapons in the arsenal of the colonials during the Revolution. Early in the war John Trumbull, one of the Connecticut Wits, recounted in his mock-epic *M'Fingal* (1782) the vicissitudes of a Tory squire who becomes so obnoxious to his neighbors that they tar and feather him at a Whig rally. Francis Hopkinson, a signer of the Declaration of Independence, satirized the British, as did Philip Freneau, rightly called the poet of the Revolution.

But the folk did not have to depend entirely on the educated writers for humor. They began to invent for themselves. The American exaggeration in tale-telling appears early. Explorers and travelers exaggerated in their accounts of the New World, and the habit may have been learned from them. Franklin slyly used the technique of the tall tale in his famous letter of 1765 defending the right of the colonists to manufacture their own goods. Englishmen had objected that the wool produced in the colonies in a whole year was not sufficient to provide a pair of stockings to each inhabitant. Franklin corrected this untruth. "The very Tails of the American Sheep are so laden with Wooll, that each has a little Car or Waggon on four little wheels, to support and keep it from trailing on the Ground."

Late in the eighteenth century country folk were provided with humor by various almanacs, the most famous of which was the *Farmer's Almanack,* begun by R. B. Thomas in 1793. Earlier almanac advice had been dispensed in standard upper-class prose. Thomas had the brilliant idea of writing his moral essays in farmer speech and giving his characters country names. In the early 1800's a sale of a hundred thousand copies of an issue was not unusual. As *Old Farmer's Almanac,* it is still being published.

In the early years of the Republic dramatists, poets, and novelists were engaged in a deliberate effort to create an "American" literature which should, through the use of native settings, characters, and themes, declare our literary independence from Great Britain. The stage Yankee appeared first in Royall Tyler's *The Contrast* (1787), in the person of a servant, Jonathan. He owed something to the yokels of British drama, but he is an authentic creation by a New Englander who knew the type. The Negro in these early plays is always, of course, a farcical character. By this time there were enough Irish immigrants in the country to make the bog-trotter and his brogue recognizable. The comic frontier roarer arrived late, in the 1831 production of James Kirke Paulding's *The Lion of the West.*

Washington Irving's first work, "Letters of Jonathan Oldstyle, Gent." (1802–3), showed that he was aware of laughter-provoking social distinctions in American life. His Diedrich Knickerbocker's *A History of New York* (1809) is the first piece of sustained comic writing in America. Though it is in some respects genuine history, Irving's main purpose was to burlesque pompous learning.

To Irving belongs the credit of having propagated the humorous sketch, part autobiography, part gentle observation of men and manners. For more than a century it was a staple of the magazines. Much of Nathaniel Hawthorne's early writing is in this genre: "Fire Worship" (fireplaces vs. stoves), "Chippings with a Chisel" (conversations with a carver of gravestones), and, at a higher level, the satirical allegories, "Earth's Holocaust" and "The Celestial Railroad."

Fenimore Cooper was a humorless man, but he knew that a novel required humor characters and he did his best to conform. In *The Spy* (1821) the Negro Caesar Thompson and Betty Flanagan, the innkeeper, are somewhat mechanically introduced, but Maria Edgeworth observed of Betty that "an Irish pen could not have drawn her better" and Caesar is the first careful portrait of a Negro in American literature. The humorous characters in *The Pioneers* (1823) were observed at first hand. Cooper had known them as a boy in semi-frontier Cooperstown – New Englanders, Mohawk Valley Germans, and rovers from Britain and the West Indies.

At the beginning of his career Edgar Allan Poe thought of himself as a poet and had little respect for serious fiction. In many of his earlier prose pieces he attempted humor and satire of various kinds: hoaxes, satirical fantasies, burlesques of pedantic language and of contemporary styles in fiction, such as "Hans Pfaall," "Four Beasts in One, or The Homo-Camelopard," and "The Literary Life of Thingum Bob, Esq." Poe called these pieces "grotesques."

Though these and many other early American writers made incidental use of humor, the professional humorist did not arrive on the scene until the 1830's. The men who first made humor their business developed patterns or modes which persisted for a century. Almost all of them invented humorous characters whose doings and sayings, in installments, were capable of amusing the public for years. During the 1830's and 1840's both the North and the South produced professional humorists in abundance. Chronologically the North has a slight priority. Seba Smith's *The Life and Writings of Major Jack Downing, of Downingville, Away Down East in the State of Maine* was published in 1833, two years before the first collection of humorous tales was issued in the South: Augustus Baldwin Longstreet's *Georgia Scenes.*

Seba Smith was valedictorian of his class at Bowdoin College, but he knew the rural Down East life which he depicted in Jack's letters. Downingville is a composite of the villages in the Sebago Lake region in which the Smith family had lived. Young Jack's adventures begin when he comes to Portland to seek his fortune, bringing with him as capital one dollar, a load of ax handles, a cheese, and cousin Nabby's bundle of footings. He marvels at city ways and is fascinated by party strife in the Maine legislature. He decides forthwith to become a politician. Defeated as candidate for governor, he goes on foot to Washington City to see if he can help President Jackson who is having trouble with his Cabinet. In no time at all Jack is Old Hickory's confidant.

Smith's characters, Jack himself and his many relatives – father and mother, Cousin Ephraim and Uncle Joshua (a local politician and a sharp trader) – are well differentiated in their speech and in the observations they make. Smith reproduces Down East speech excellently, relying more on cadence and turns of phrase than on phonetic or eccentric spelling. In the first letters Jack is the Yankee bumpkin, but he learns fast and accepts modestly the great honors and responsibilities which come his way. The humor is so unforced that it almost seems as if Jack had really been an intimate of the General.

Smith's Major Jack was so popular that he was frequently imitated. The most annoying to Smith of the plagiarists was Charles Augustus Davis of New York whose *Letters of J. Downing, Major, Downingville Militia* (1834) may have been more widely known than the Smith originals. Another imitator, though at a distance, was a Canadian, Judge Thomas Chandler Haliburton of Nova Scotia. His comic Yankee, Sam Slick the Clockmaker, is much inferior to Smith's Major but he made a great hit in Canada, England, and America although Haliburton had invented him merely as a device for commenting on the backwardness of Canada in developing its natural resources. The three series of Sam Slick letters (1836, 1838, 1840) have little plan and Haliburton disguises the fact that he had no ear for genuine Yankee speech by Sam's ceaseless story-telling and smart-trading. Sam Slick probably appealed so widely because he incarnated the Yankee of the popular imagination.

The first female comic figure – also a Yankee – was Frances M. Whitcher's Widow Bedott. While the good widow is angling (successfully) for a second husband, she occupies her spare time with morning calls, donation parties, and the activities of the sewing circle. Her observations began appearing in the magazines in the 1840's and were collected as *The Widow Bedott Papers* in 1855. Even more popular than the widow was Benjamin Penhallow Shillaber's Mrs. Partington. She was invented in 1847 and had a long life through her *Life and Sayings* (1854) and *Knitting Work* (1859). For humor Shillaber relied on malapropisms ("Apollyon Bonypart," "Mount Vociferous"), pithy sayings, and subsidiary characters who stir up Mrs. P.'s comments on such contemporary phenomena as spirit-rapping and the Maine Law, our first experiment in prohibition.

James Russell Lowell turned professional humorist in the 1840's and again in the early years of the Civil War. As a devoted son of New England, he was much interested in the Yankee vernacular and its possibilities in verse-making. (Burns hovers in the background here.) This interest, combined with Lowell's strong anti-slavery feelings and his disgust with the Mexican War (to him "the slave-holders' war"), produced *The Biglow Papers* (1848). To promulgate his ideas Lowell invented the semiliterate Hosea Biglow whose abilities at versifying are encouraged by his Whiggish pastor, Parson Wilbur. When passing on to the newspapers Hosea's verses, Wilbur sends along each time his own (prose) comment on the poem. Lowell invented a third character, to get in still another New England type, Birdofredom Sawin, a Yankee clown who has been gulled into enlisting and can thus send back from Mexico firsthand reports of battles and yellow fever and the insolence of officers. When the Civil War began Lowell's northern sympathies induced him to revive his three characters to propagandize for the Union cause, but the second series of poems (1867) is inferior to the first. *The Biglow Papers* are not easy reading today, chiefly because they are densely topical. But none of these inventors of Yankee humor had a keener ear for Yankee speech than Lowell and he took great pains to record it exactly.

The humor produced in the old Southwest was far more vigorous than that turned out by the professional humorists in the North. In the great migration into the Mississippi Territory between 1800 and 1830 were all sorts of men, from sober citizens who intended to carve out plantations to confidence men and claim jumpers. Life was often hard but it was seldom dull. The southern humorists would clearly never run out of materials.

In his introduction to *Tall Tales of the Southwest* Franklin J. Meine sums up the subjects available: courtships and weddings; law circuits and political life; sports, from horse racing to coon hunts; oddities of character; travel (particularly steamboat life on the Mississippi); frontier medical practice; gambling; camp meetings and religious revivals; fights. The humor based on these activities ranged all the way from the mild satire of provincial manners, in W. T. Thompson's Major Jones stories, to the brutal horseplay of George W. Harris' Sut Lovingood and the macabre medical experiments of "Madison Tensas, the Louisiana Swamp Doctor" (pseudonym of Henry Clay Lewis).

As in the North, many of these humorists were newspapermen. Some were lawyers, who picked up local stories as they followed the judge on circuit in the days when court was likely to be convened in the back room of the crossroads doggery (i.e., combined grocery store and saloon). The career of George W. Harris is representative. He was successively a silversmith, riverboat captain, inventor, metal-worker, postmaster, and business adventurer. Along the way he invented Sut Lovingood.

These humorists are not to be identified with their characters. They were not clayeaters or Georgia Crackers nor did they indulge in gouging fights. Most of them were self-educated, though A. B. Longstreet and T. B. Thorpe were college trained. All of them were aware of the long tradition of humor writing. In recent studies their gentility has been stressed, as a corrective to earlier views. But it must be remembered that they had thrown in their lot with the semi-frontier South they described. The raffish behavior which they observed amused them and they made it amusing to their readers.

Their stories and sketches appeared first in the local papers. The best of them were spotted by editors in the North who helped themselves freely. As the fame of these writers spread, their work was collected in book form. The chief promoter of southern humor was William T. Porter, a Vermonter who in 1831 established in New York a sporting magazine, *Spirit of the Times,* modeled on *Bell's Life in London.* Because he was a great admirer of southern humor, Porter's journal soon became as much a magazine of humor as of sport.

The pioneer among the southern humorists was Augustus Baldwin Longstreet. His "Georgia Scenes" appeared first in Milledgeville and Augusta newspapers. In 1835 he issued them in book form from the office of the Augusta *States Rights Sentinel,* which he owned. *Georgia Scenes* was immediately popular in the North (where Harper reissued it in 1840) as well as the South. Georgians, who had long suffered from the cultural condescension of Virginia and South Carolina, were proud to have a famous book they could call their own.

The "characters, incidents, &c" promised on the title page furnish a conspectus of the varieties of southern humor. Among the incidents are a horse-swap, an ear-and-nose-biting fight, a fox hunt, a shooting match, and a gander-pulling. (The winner in this sporting event successfully yanks off the greased neck of the gander as he comes full tilt at the bird suspended from a rig.) Not all of Longstreet's sketches deal with low life. Seven of the eighteen are about genteel folk.

As a young lawyer on circuit, Longstreet had enjoyed to the full the life of the followers of the court. He was known, even at Yale, as a wonderful storyteller, and there was a natural demand to have his stories in print. When he collected them, the future parson and college president was careful to inform readers who might object to his occasional use of "coarse, inelegant, and sometimes ungrammatical language" that such speech is "accommodated to the capacity of the person" who is speaking. To distance himself from his more boorish characters Longstreet uses a framing device which many of the southern humorists adopted. The introducer of the story stands aside and lets the teller speak for himself. This device got the introducer off the hook, if he was wary of objections from genteel readers. It also permitted him, if he was a Whig — and he usually was — to dissent subtly from the "Democratic" behavior of his characters.

One of Longstreet's first imitators was William T. Thompson, who had been associated with him in editing the Augusta *Sentinel*. Thompson's principal creation is Major Jones of Pineville, whom he sends through a long courtship, providing him at last with a wife and baby and a plantation. The Major appears first in *Major Jones's Courtship* (1843). The story and the satire move slowly along by means of letters which the Major permits Mr. Thompson to print in the papers. Encouraged by the success of his first volume, Thompson brushed up some of his earlier tales which he hoped might furnish "interesting specimens of the genus 'Cracker' " and collected them in *Major Jones's Chronicles of Pineville* (1845). In *Major Jones's Sketches of Travel* (1847) the Major journeys to Washington City, New York, Niagara Falls, and Quebec, commenting on the wonders he sees and the strange ways of the people he meets.

Two other southern humorists invented characters whose adventures are recorded in related stories. But Thompson's Major is a milksop compared to Johnson J. Hooper's picaro, Simon Suggs, and George W. Harris' Sut Lovingood, that "nat'ral born durn'd fool" from East Tennessee.

Born in North Carolina, Hooper moved to the Alabama frontier when the fortunes of his family declined. A lawyer by profession, he soon began contributing Whiggish editorials to the *East Alabamian.* His first story, "Taking the Census" (1843), was based on his experiences in trying to extract vital statistics from suspicious country people during the census-taking of 1840. Late in the next year came the first Simon Suggs story. Porter spotted Hooper's talent and began reprinting his pieces in the *Spirit of the Times.*

Suggs's career as a rogue begins early. While still a "shirt-tail boy" he steals his mother's roosters to fight them at Bob Smith's grocery and his father's plow horses to enter them in quarter matches. When his preacher father tries to put a stop to his card-playing, young Simon tells him it's no use to try. "I'm gwine to play cards as long as I live. When I go off to myself, I'm gwine to make my livin' by it. So what's the use of beatin' me about it?" Suggs's motto is "It's good to be shifty in a new country" and he acts accordingly. He collects money on false pretenses from a claim filer, passes himself off as a rich uncle, and steals the collection money at a camp meeting after proving himself to be the most eloquent exhorter of the session.

When Hooper gathered the Suggs stories as *Some Adventures of Captain Simon Suggs* (1845), he pretended he was offering a campaign biography. Suggs thinks it "more than probable he shall come before the people of Tallapoosa [County] in the course of a year or two." Naturally the voters, or at least all good Democrats, will want to have his biography. Though Hooper wrote many tales not in the Suggs cycle (most of them were collected in a volume of 1851), nothing that he wrote surpassed the adventures of his Captain Suggs, "late of the Tallapoosa volunteers."

Harris' Sut Lovingood is an even more brilliant creation than Simon Suggs. In Sut's storytelling southern humor reaches its high-water mark. Sut is the prince of practical jokers. He puts lizards up the pantlegs of the parson while he is preaching about the "sarpints in hell." He breaks up a wedding by sending a bull and a beehive into the ceremony. He frightens an Irishman out of town by tying a hog-gut to his shirttail while he is asleep. When Sut's victim wakes up, he thinks a snake has crawled into bed with him. Sut is loudmouthed, sex-ridden, and brutal, but he is a great storyteller. Harris also gave him the gift of language, in the words he uses, his turns of phrase, and his metaphors.

When the Lovingood tales were collected in 1867, Sut asked "George" to say in the preface that "this yere perduckshun" will not "sit purfeckly quiet ontu the stumicks ove sum pussons – them hu hes a holesum fear ove the devil, an' orter hev hit, by geminey. . . . Ef yu ain't fond ove the smell ove cracklins, stay outen the kitchin; ef yu is fear'd ove smut, yu needn't climb the chimbley; an' ef the moon hurts yer eyes, don't yu ever look at a Dutch cheese." Enough readers have relished the smell of Sut's cracklins to keep *Sut Lovingood. Yarns Spun by a 'Nat'ral Born Durn'd Fool.' Warped and Wove for Public Wear* in print almost continuously since 1867.

One of the most admired of contributors to the *Spirit of the Times* was Thomas B. Thorpe, portrait painter, soldier-reporter in the Mexican War, and editor. His tales and sketches were collected in *The Mysteries of the Backwoods* (1846) and *The Hive of the Bee Hunter* (1854). Thorpe was a northerner who fell in love with southern scenery, sports, and tall-talk. His detailed reports on "Arrow-Fishing," "Alligator Killing," and "Buffalo Hunting" were as much liked as his stories. The most famous of his tales is "The Big Bear of Arkansas" which had been widely reprinted before he put it into his *Hive of the Bee Hunter.* The teller is the man who killed the Big Bear, a fabulous critter who had defied all dogs and bullets. The story is the best tall tale to come out of the Southwest, for Thorpe lifts his story above the expected exaggerations to the level of myth. A sense of mystery and awe remains with the teller: "My private opinion is, that that bear was an *unhuntable bear, and died when his time come.*"

Many of the tall tales of the Southwest which were circulated orally before they got into print were eventually attached to the two principal folk heroes of the region, Mike Fink and Davy Crockett. Mike operated on three frontiers: as a scout in the Indian country around Pittsburgh, as a keelboatman on the Mississippi, and, briefly, as a mountain man in the Rockies. The first of the Mike Fink stories was printed in 1828. By the end of the century more than seventy had appeared.

Davy Crockett is a more substantial figure because he was for a time in national politics and took a hand in manufacturing the Crockett legend. Having served two terms in the Tennessee legislature, Crockett was elected to Congress in 1827. His break with Jackson gave the Whigs a welcome opportunity to exploit him as a genuine backwoodsman and bear-hunter who had deserted Jacksonian Democracy. Whig propagandists did most of the work of building up the Crockett legend though Davy (with the assistance of a ghost-writer) published in 1834 his *Narrative of the Life of David Crockett, of the State of Tennessee.* As the books about Crockett multiplied (their authorship is still a tangle of conjecture), the anecdotes spilled over into the Crockett almanacs. Some fifty of these appeared in at least a half-dozen cities between 1835 and 1856. The makers of the almanacs vied with one another in tying up to Davy any good frontier story they could get their hands on. When the Crockett almanacs were rescued from oblivion in the 1930's they proved to be one of the richest stores of southwestern humor we have.

Much of the Down East and southwestern humor continued to be enjoyed in the latter half of the nineteenth century. The works of Smith, Lowell, Longstreet, and Thompson were kept in print and, as we have seen, Harris' Sut Lovingood tales survived into this century. Only the brutal medical stories of the "Louisiana Swamp Doctor" dropped from sight.

In the 1850's and 1860's a new brand of humor began to flourish. By the end of the Civil War the "literary comedians" who produced it (the term was first applied to them in 1890) were nationally known. The books which established their reputations appeared in this order: "John Phoenix" (George H. Derby), *Phoenixiana*, 1856; "Orpheus C. Kerr" (Robert Henry Newell), *The Orpheus C. Kerr Papers*, 1862; "Artemus Ward" (Charles Farrar Browne), *Artemus Ward; His Book*, 1862; "Petroleum V. Nasby" (David Ross Locke), *The Nasby Papers*, 1864; "Private Miles O'Reilly" (Charles G. Halpine), *The Life and Adventures . . . of Private Miles O'Reilly*, 1864; "Josh Billings" (Henry W. Shaw), *Josh Billings, His Sayings*, 1865; and "Bill Arp" (Charles H. Smith), *Bill Arp, So-Called*, 1866. Derby, Browne and Halpine died in the 1860's but the others lived a long time and wrote a great deal. A latecomer was "Bill Nye" (Edgar Wilson Nye) whose *Bill Nye and Boomerang*, the first of twelve books, appeared in 1881. These eight men are the best and most popular of the literary comedians. Once they had proved how profitable a business humor-writing for a nation-wide audience could be, they had a crowd of imitators.

Much of this humor has lost its savor, but there is no need to condescend to such pieces (there are not many of them, I will grant) as Ward's "A Visit to Brigham Young," Phoenix's "Musical Review Extraordinary," or Kerr's burlesque of the surrender terms Grant offered Lee.

One notices first that their humor is seldom regional. This is true even of George H. Derby, an easterner who settled in California. His best pieces – such as the (burlesque) "Lectures on Astronomy" and "A New System of English Grammar" – have no western flavor. The humorists moved about the country, especially when they took to the lecture platform, and they picked up their material wherever they could find it. Since they wanted a national audience, they could not afford to satirize local affairs. Gone, too, is the occasional brutality of the humor which appeared in Porter's *Spirit of the Times,* a magazine which a lady would have blushed to read.

This new humor is closely identified with the carefully built up character of the narrator. "Artemus Ward" is speaking, not Charles Farrar Browne; "Josh Billings," not Henry Wheeler Shaw. These pseudonymous talkers were the puppets of their creators. Only occasionally did the puppeteer project himself into the show. Just who was doing the talking sometimes confused the public, particularly when the humorists began to tour on the lyceum circuit. Browne first presented his creation in print as a spieler for a waxworks show. Many people who came to hear a lecture by Artemus Ward expected to see the show and hear "Artemus" explain it to them. What they heard was "The Babes in the Woods" or "Sixty Minutes in Africa," comic lectures delivered deadpan by a neatly dressed man whose voice, it is reported, was "clear, sweet, and pleasant" and whose manner was "attractive and agreeable."

The literary comedians created few characters beside the puppets through whom they talked. Possibly in this fact lies the greatest difference between the newer humor and the older. Seba Smith brought Major Jack Downing's numerous relatives into the act and gave them much to do and say in their own right. Josh Billings has no parents, uncles, or cousins.

These new humorists relied almost entirely on tricks of language to get laughs. Their humor was verbal humor. The effect most of them tried to produce was that of a shrewd illiteracy. Much of the fun came from the absurd incongruity of sharp comments on people and events rendered in bad spelling, misused words, fractured grammar, mixed metaphors, pretentious and misapplied learning. The outrageous spelling, which is tedious to us now, was a subtle form of flattery. By 1850 most Americans could spell. (With Artemus Ward bad spelling was more than a trick. It is usually phonetic and we hear in it Browne's native Maine speech.) Since this humor was verbal, the forms used were varieties of the takeoff: spoof reporting, abusive letters to the editor, travel sketches full of irrelevancies, burlesques of sermons, orations, historical writing, sentimental fiction, and the lyceum lecture.

The burlesque lecture enriched Browne, Shaw, Locke, Nye, Mark Twain, and many others. Locke boasted that he made during his first lecture season the longest and most lucrative tour in the annals of the lyceum. In the nine months he was on the road he took in $30,000. Robert Jones Burdette of Iowa is said to have delivered his "Rise and Fall of the Moustache" over 5000 times. The point of the comic lecture was that it had no point. Josh Billings' lecture on "Milk" never referred to the announced subject, though a glass of milk was solemnly placed on the podium before Josh began to pour down his shower of epigrams.

In a span of seven years Mark Twain established himself as the best of the literary comedians. When Artemus Ward died in 1867, Twain, then thirty-two, was spoken of as his successor though his first full-length work, *The Innocents Abroad,* would not be published until 1869. This is not the place to review the major works of Mark Twain (there is a pamphlet devoted to him in this series) but something must be said about how he became a professional humorist and the traditions which nourished his art.

Twain's course was fixed in the spring of 1862 when he began contributing letters signed "Josh" to the *Territorial Enterprise* of Virginia City, Nevada. In August he became a reporter and feature writer for the paper, filling his required two columns with more fiction than fact. In October came the first hint of fame when his journalistic hoax, a report of the "discovery" of a petrified man, was widely circulated as a true story. This kind of burlesque reporting was just what the miners on the Comstock Lode wanted. Another decisive moment in his climb to fame as a humorist was the visit of Artemus Ward to Virginia City in December 1863. The famous humorist and the young reporter hit it off wonderfully. Mark had a hero to emulate.

Twain left Nevada in May 1864 and settled in San Francisco, where he worked for two papers. Here he spent much of his time in the company of two other humorists, Bret Harte and Robert Henry Newell. Two events in 1865 impelled him further along his appointed course. Ward had invited him to contribute to *Artemus Ward, His Travels.* The story he prepared, "The Celebrated Jumping Frog of Calaveras County," arrived too late to be included, but it was printed in the New York *Saturday Press* and other papers. James Russell Lowell pronounced it "the finest piece of humorous literature yet produced in America." Also in November, Twain went to the Sandwich Islands as a correspondent of the Sacramento *Union.* His travel letters, part straight reporting, part humor, added to his growing repertory.

In 1866 Twain made his first appearances as a comic lecturer. Though he worried over this venture, he had no reason to be apprehensive. The San Francisco *Bulletin* said of the first lecture that it was superior to Artemus Ward's "The Babes in the Woods": "as a humorous writer Mark Twain stands in the foremost rank." Meanwhile the *Alta California* (of San Francisco) had commissioned Twain to go on the *Quaker City* excursion to Europe and the Holy Land (one of the first luxury cruises) and report the reactions of these latter-day pilgrims to Old World culture. The New York *Tribune* also arranged to print his travel letters. When Twain left California in December 1866, he was headed east to stay.

The *Quaker City* letters received wide newspaper circulation. When Twain again took to the lecture platform, late in 1868, with his "American Vandal Abroad" lecture, his fame had traveled ahead of him. For the first few minutes of the lecture some listeners were fooled by the studied slow speech, the drawl, the low-keyed humor, the impassive face into believing they were in for an evening of boredom. But, as an Indianapolis reporter observed, the awakening came suddenly, and the doubter was soon "a willing and delighted captive, drinking in every word."

In these years Twain worked within the conventions of the humorists contemporary with him. He welcomed Artemus Ward to Virginia City in Ward's own style. Artemus was coming, Mark said, to "sekure a kupple ov horned todes; alsowe a lizard which it may be persessed of 2 tales, or any komical snaix." Twain burlesqued everything in sight which needed burlesquing: women's fashions, spiritualism, sports reporting ("The Great Prize Fight" —between Governor Stanford and Governor-Elect Low), melodrama (" 'Ingomar' over the Mountains"), society reporting ("The Lick House Ball"). The "Jumping Frog" story was a frontier tall tale which had circulated in the mining camps. In his comic lectures he followed the example of Artemus Ward, mixing together a few verifiable facts, anecdotes, and items of autobiography and inventing a stage personality to hold the parts together.

Twain was venturing where his predecessors had gone but in time he ventured much farther. He was the only literary comedian whose skill in storytelling led him to attempt full-length fiction. The turn came, probably, when he wrote "Old Times on the Mississippi" for the *Atlantic Monthly* in 1875. He had begun to feel that he was at a dead end. His rediscovery of the "Matter of the River" revealed to him its possibilities for fiction. A year after the *Atlantic* articles came *The Adventures of Tom Sawyer*. Though *The Adventures of Huckleberry Finn* was not finished until 1883, Huck's potential importance was clear to Twain when he wrote the last pages of *Tom Sawyer*.

Twain's most significant discovery was the immense resources for the writer of fiction in the American vernacular. Other humorists, eastern, southern, western, had recognized in the speech of ordinary Americans only the fun to be made of it and from it. Twain learned how to make a great novel, by turns realistic, funny, angry, pathetic, serious to the verge of tragedy, from the words of Tom and Nigger Jim, of Pap and the King and the Duke.

The literary comedians made almost no use of dialect but dialect humor flourished during the time of their ascendancy. As the tide of immigration flooded into the country in the second half of the century, another group of writers saw the possibilities of humor in the struggles the new arrivals were having with American ways and the American language. Dialect humor was for many years a staple in the humor magazines, but it did not survive World War I. The sons and daughters of the immigrants had been rapidly absorbed into the national life and they objected to Pat and Mike stories or poems about beer-guzzling Germans who said "giss" for kiss and "troonk" for drunk.

The writers of dialect humor knew that there would be objections and prepared to meet them in different ways. When Charles Godfrey Leland collected his Hans Breitmann ballads in one volume he was careful to say this in his preface: "If Teutonic philosophy and sentiment, beer, music, and romance, have been made the medium for what many reviewers have kindly declared to be laughter-moving, let the reader be assured that not a single word was meant in a bitter or unkindly spirit." Finley Peter Dunne took a different line with the organizers of a movement to drive Irish jokes off the stage and out of the press. To an editor who wished to defend Dunne's "Mr. Dooley" he wrote in 1903: "I hope you will not bother your head or disturb the symmetry of your paper by attempting a defense of me against these bootblacks. Let them howl."

Leland was not prepared for the great popularity of his "Hans Breitmann's Barty," the first of the Breitmann ballads. He wrote it as a filler for *Graham's Magazine* of which he was the editor in 1857. Leland was an able linguist – he later made studies of gypsy life, tinkers' language, and Italian witch lore – and his knowledge of German had been perfected in the three years he spent in German universities. Hans is a huge, bearded German-American whose reputation for drinking was fixed in the ballad about his "barty." The popularity of the Breitmann ballads compelled Leland to go on writing them for nearly forty years.

The Irish-American was a comic figure on the stage before the Civil War and every vaudeville and burlesque show in later years offered at least one Irish comedian. But the greatest Irish-American comic is Finley Peter Dunne's Mr. Dooley. Dunne, who was Irish himself, invented Mr. Dooley, the philosophical barkeep, and his stooge-friend Mr. Hennessy of Archey Road to project his opinions about Chicago politics and business life and national affairs. Dunne's radical social views would not otherwise have got past the newspaper owners for whom he worked. Mr. Dooley's principal targets are civic corruption, from City Hall to the United States Senate, and American chauvinism at the time of the Spanish-American War. Some of the Dooley pieces are as fresh as ever; for instance, Mr. Dooley's description of the effect on Teddy Roosevelt's digestion of Upton Sinclair's *The Jungle,* a novel about the filthy conditions in the Chicago meat-packing factories, and his comment on the Supreme Court decisions in 1901, with its famous punch line, "No matther whether th' Constitution follows th' flag or not, th' Supreme Coort follows th' iliction returns."

Little was done before the twentieth century to alter the picture of the Jewish immigrant as a sharp trader in baggy pants. There was a rich tradition of Yiddish humor but not much of it was available in English. Montague Glass, an English Jew who had come to America in 1890, introduced his famous partners in the cloak and suit business, Abe and Mawruss, in *Potash & Perlmutter* (1910). More books about Abe and Mawruss followed and they made several stage appearances. Jewish dialect humor survives, perhaps because Jews generally do not object to it and like to tell Jewish stories themselves. Otherwise the *New Yorker* would not have risked Arthur Kober's stories about the Gross family or the sketches of Leo C. Rosten, collected in 1937 as *The Education of H*y*m*a*n K*a*p*l*a*n.*

The Negroes were our first immigrant aliens, in the sense that they were from the beginning felt to be an alien element in a population made up almost entirely of immigrants. The plantation slaves had their own orally transmitted humor which their white owners persisted in believing was carefree and high-spirited. They missed the sly deceptions and covert protests in the slaves' work songs. Some of these were also heard, strangely enough, in the immensely popular minstrel shows, for blackface minstrelsy was not entirely a travesty of Negro life.

Joel Chandler Harris, chief editorial writer of the Atlanta *Constitution* for many years, combined in his Uncle Remus stories the usual southern image of the kindly old Uncle Tom with the

Negro's desire to triumph over the white man, in fantasy at least. As a boy Harris had lived on a plantation where the slaves were well treated and had heard from them the Negro folktales he would later put in the mouth of Uncle Remus. An article on "Folklore of Southern Negroes," printed in *Lippincott's Magazine* in 1877, gave Harris his cue. The first Uncle Remus tale – "The Story of Mr. Rabbit and Mr. Fox" – appeared in the *Constitution* in July, 1879. The famous Tar Baby story was the second in the series. Within a year Harris had accumulated enough stories to make the first of his Uncle Remus books – *Uncle Remus, His Songs and Sayings*. Nine more collections were to follow.

There are two partially concealed strains in the stories. Harris' paper was pro-New South, but he himself had doubts about progress through industrialization and he occasionally uses Uncle Remus as a mask through which to voice them. More significant is Harris' awareness that Brer Rabbit's victories over Brer Fox are fables of the Negro's ability to cheat his master or escape punishment. As he wrote in the introduction to the first collection of stories, "It needs no scientific investigation to show why [the Negro] selects as his hero the weakest and most harmless of all animals, and brings him out victorious in contests with the bear, the wolf, and the fox." Most readers missed these implications, and the general effect of the Uncle Remus stories was a sentimental picture of plantation life. For this reason the modern Negro dislikes them, and they may not survive.

Mark Twain prefaced *The Adventures of Huckleberry Finn* with this note: "In this book a number of dialects are used, to wit: the Missouri negro dialect; the extremest form of the backwoods Southwestern dialect; the ordinary 'Pike County' dialect; and four modified varieties of this last. The shadings have not been done in a haphazard fashion, or by guesswork; but painstakingly, and with the trustworthy guidance and support of personal familiarity with these several forms of speech."

Few readers, one supposes, caught all seven of these shadings, but by this date many writers of fiction had discovered, as Twain did, the possibilities for the revelation of character through dialect and had begun to explore the gamut of the American vernacular. The tag "local color" has been attached to this new variety of fiction. It is an unsatisfactory term because it gives little indication of the richness of the stories subsumed under the label. Any discussion of American humor must take account of them because most of them were humorous in intent.

The local-color short stories were just what the newer literary magazines – the *Atlantic Monthly, Lippincott's,* and *Scribner's* – were looking for, something fresh and novel. Several of these magazines had a very wide circulation, and so the local-color stories were presented to a large audience. Within ten years of the war's end every region had been heard from. Bret Harte, an easterner who had gone to California in 1854, began turning out his "Pike" dialect stories in the late 1860's. His first collection, *The Luck of Roaring Camp and Other Sketches* (1870), was phenomenally successful. Harriet Beecher Stowe's *Oldtown Folks,* stories and sketches based on the boyhood experiences of her Massachusetts-born minister husband, appeared in 1869. When Edward Eggleston published *The Hoosier Schoolmaster* in 1871 he said in his preface that it had been a matter of no little jealousy with him "that the manners, customs, thoughts, and feelings of New England country people filled so large a place in books, while our life, not less interesting, not less romantic, and certainly not less filled with humorous and grotesque material, had no place in literature." He had had it in mind since boyhood "to do something toward describing life in the back-country districts of the Western States." Sarah Orne Jewett's first book, *Deephaven* (1877), served the same purpose for the decaying port villages of southern Maine. Meanwhile in New Orleans, George Washington Cable, returned from the war, wrote about the Creole folkways which were slowly dissolving under the "go-ahead" spirit of *les Américains* on the other side of Canal Street. In their effort to write realistically, though certainly not naturalistically, about the people they knew, the regionalists found the ability to manipulate dialect for humorous effects to be one of their principal assets.

Connections between local-color fiction, with its emphasis on the incongruous, the quaint, and the humorous, and earlier and contemporary humor are readily apparent. Many of the fiction writers were or had been writers of humorous poems or sketches. It was easy for George W. Bagby, the Virginia journalist, to move from his letters of "Mozis Addums" (a southern Jack Downing), contributed to the *Southern Literary Messenger* in 1858, to the humorous sketches and local-color stories collected in *The Old Virginia Gentleman*. Bret Harte was a professional humorist before he turned to fiction. His *Condensed Novels* (1867) contains some of the best burlesques of fiction (Cooper, Dumas, Charlotte Brontë, Dickens) written in the century. One section of his *Poems* (1871) is given over to humorous dialect poems, the best of which is the much-liked "Plain Language from Truthful James," a tale of the biter bitten by a "naive" Chinese immigrant. In an article on the rise of the short story, published in the *Cornhill Magazine* in 1899, Harte praised American humor for its originality and noted its influence on the short story. "By degrees [American humor] developed character with its incident, often, in a few lines, gave a striking photograph of a community or a section, but always reached its conclusion without an unnecessary word. . . . It was the parent of the American 'short story.' "

Another postwar development was the arrival of the humorous newspaper column. It had a vigorous existence for sixty years during which time many of the columnists became national figures. Their work was usually syndicated and the best of it later appeared in book form. The shrewdest of them manipulated their copyrights the way a broker deals in stocks. Frank M. ("Kin") Hubbard, whose Brown County philosopher, Abe Martin, ruminated in the Indianapolis *News,* set up his own publishing house from which eighteen Abe Martin books were issued.

Apparently the originator of the humorous column was James M. Bailey, "The Danbury News Man." When Bailey returned from the Civil War, he bought and consolidated two papers as the Danbury *News.* His column consisted of folksy stories, mostly about domestic crises and the pranks of small boys. He also inserted news items burlesquing the "personals" printed in small-town papers. Bailey's collection of his pieces, *Life in Danbury,* sold 33,000 copies in eleven weeks. Robert Jones Burdette's column, "Hawk-eyetems of Roaming Robert," was a feature of the Burlington (Iowa) *Daily Hawk-Eye* in the early seventies. About the same time "M. Quad" (Charles Bertrand Lewis) began a column in the Detroit *Free Press* which he conducted for nearly twenty years before moving to the New York *World.*

The humor of Eugene Field is more sophisticated than that of these earlier columnists. We begin to see in it the sharp comment on public figures of the kind that characterized the writing of such a later columnist as Heywood Broun. Field's first column appeared in the Denver *Tribune* (1881–83). The book which was compiled from it, *The Tribune Primer,* has life in it still in such acidulous sketches as "The Baby" and "The Editor's Valise." In 1883 Field moved to Chicago where he wrote his "Sharps and Flats" column for the *Record* until his death in 1895. It was a miscellany of topical commentary, a good deal of it on writers, and humorous and sentimental verse, in which infant mortality was very high. Needless to say none of Field's bawdy poems, which delighted his friends, strayed into "Sharps and Flats."

When George Ade was hired by the Chicago *Record*, one of his duties was to fill two columns in each issue with a feature called "Stories of the Streets and of the Town." In the issue of September 17, 1897, he printed a piece labeled "This Is a Fable," the first of the soon to be famous Fables in Slang. When these were first collected in 1900 nearly 70,000 copies were sold within the year. The Fables were a new departure in American humor. "M. Quad" had introduced some "American Fables" into his column but they were imitations of Aesop with only a slight "American" flavor. Ade's purpose was to ridicule middle-class complacency, respectability, and social timidity, as the titles show: "The Fable of the Parents Who Tinkered with the Offspring"; "The Fable of Flora and Adolph and a Home Gone Wrong"; "The Fable of the Honest Money-Maker and the Partner of his Joys, Such as They Were."

Chicago was the proving ground of humor columnists. "B. L. T." (Bert Leston Taylor) invented "A Line-o'-Type or Two" for the Chicago *Tribune* where it was a feature of the editorial page for nearly twenty years. "F. P. A." (Franklin P. Adams) wrote his first column for the *Journal* in 1903, moving on to the New York *Evening Mail* the next year. His "Conning Tower" column began appearing in the New York *Tribune* in 1913.

The most inventive of the later columnists was Don Marquis whose first column, "The Sun Dial," was introduced in the New York *Evening Sun* in 1912. When he went to the *Tribune* in 1922, he named his new column "The Lantern." Marquis did not usually write about himself or his friends or comment directly on the state of the nation. The characters he invented spoke for him. The most popular of these were archy the giant cockroach and his friend mehitabel the alley cat. Marquis discovered archy one morning jumping about on the keys of the typewriter. "He could not work the capital letters, and he had a great deal of difficulty operating the mechanism that shifts the paper so that a fresh line may be started. We never saw a cockroach work so hard or perspire so freely in all our lives before." He had typed out a poem. It begins

> expression is the need of my soul
> i was once a vers libre bard
> but i died and my soul went into the body of a cockroach
> it has given me a new outlook upon life.

The boss continued to receive reports from archy on his experiences in the worm and insect world and the progress of his friendship with mehitabel, whose spirit was formerly "incarnated in the body of cleopatra."

Walter Blair observes that humorous columns "gradually became unfashionable and tended to be replaced by those made up of serious commentary, gossip or feature stories." We can note further that as the greater newspapers have permitted feature writers to comment freely, their columns often take a humorous or witty turn. James Reston, chief Washington correspondent of the New York *Times,* for example, is as good a satirist as he is a reporter on national affairs. A few humorous columns still flourish: George Dixon's "Washington Scene" in the Washington *Post*; Art Buchwald's column in the New York *Herald Tribune*; and Russell Baker's "Observer" in the New York *Times.*

Much of the humorous writing of the nineteenth and early twentieth centuries was prepared for the humor magazines, of which some fifty were launched. Those with the longest life were *Puck* (1877–1918), *Judge* (1881–1939), and *Life* (1883–1936). The peak year was 1872 when nine comic magazines were in circulation.

The first of these magazines worth commenting on, *The Carpet-Bag,* was published in Boston between 1851 and 1853. It offered its readers several of the best humorous writers of the time. B. P. Shillaber ("Mrs. Partington") was one of the editors; among its contributors were "John Phoenix," "M. Quad," and Charles G. Halpine (not yet "Private Miles O'Reilly"). Charles Farrar Browne (not yet "Artemus Ward") came to the paper as a typesetter but was soon writing for it over the pen name "Lieutenant Chubb." The first known piece by a sixteen-year-old who signed his initials S. L. C., "The Dandy Frightening the Squatter," appeared in the issue of May 1, 1852. (Samuel Langhorne Clemens became "Mark Twain" in 1863.)

The next important arrival, *Vanity Fair* (1859–63), originated among the wits who frequented Pfaff's famous cellar-saloon on lower Broadway, but their magazine was decidedly not bohemian in tone. It was tough and bold and had a strong political bias. Its drawings, most of which were caricatures and cartoons rather than straight realism, hit hard. Though *Vanity Fair* has the look of the early *Punch,* the editors were anti-John Bull. They were also, to their cost, Democrats, though not of the Copperhead variety. The magazine probably failed because it was too critical of the national administration in wartime and made too many enemies for other reasons.

Through its early years *Puck* exhibited a split personality, but this appears to have been a strength rather than a weakness. Founded by a Viennese immigrant, Joseph Keppler, who next to Thomas Nast was the most brilliant political cartoonist of his time, *Puck* was first published as a German comic weekly. The next year (1877) an English edition, using the same colored lithographs, began its long life. (The German edition was continued for fifteen years.) The assistant editor of *Puck* in English was H. C. Bunner, one of the most suavely literate of the nineteenth-century humorists. He was soon setting the tone of the writing which appeared in the magazine. At times he wrote most of the issues himself, pouring forth an endless stream of humorous matter in prose and verse. At odds with these items and dominating them were the large, bold lithographs by Keppler, his assistants and successors, one on the cover page, a double-spread in the center of the magazine, a third on the back cover. These cartoons kept things hot for Tammany, Senator James G. Blaine, and the "Political Sodom and Gomorrah" — the two political parties. American journalism has never seen, before or since, anything like this persistent onslaught on corruption and bigotry. By the 1890's *Puck* had become more of a family magazine. Sold to Hearst's International Magazine Company in 1917, it survived only a year, though it was presenting the work of Stephen Leacock, "B. L. T.," and George Jean Nathan.

Judge was founded as the result of a secession from *Puck*, which it for some time resembled. When *Puck*'s cartoons proved helpful in the defeat of Blaine for the presidency in 1884, Republican leaders saw the necessity of having at least one humorous publication on their side. GOP money was made available and *Judge* was reorganized for this purpose. By 1912 *Judge* was ahead of *Puck* and *Life* in circulation. Some of its later contributors were S. J. Perelman, John Held, Jr., Ring Lardner, William Gropper, and Milt Gross, creator of "Nize Baby." Heywood Broun was at one time in charge of the sports department and Nathan reported on the theater. Though *Judge* bought the subscription list of *Life* in 1936 and incorporated several of *Life*'s special features into the magazine, it did not survive the depression.

Two recent graduates of Harvard, John Ames Mitchell and E. S. Martin, risked what capital they could assemble to give *Life* its start in 1883. It was slow to catch on but within a year circulation began to pick up and the long prosperity of the magazine began. *Life* was a miscellany prepared for a more sophisticated audience than the readers of *Puck* and *Judge*. It had no pronounced political bias but was strong on crusades, doing battle against the protective tariff, vivisection, the Sunday closing of museums, firecrackers, Christian Science, and Anthony Comstock. The drawings, from the beginning, were excellent. *Life*'s most successful period was in the two decades before World War I. Though it declined in prosperity and excellence after the war, it was not bankrupt when it gave up in 1936 and sold its valuable name to Time, Inc.

In the year 1925, while *Life* and *Judge* were on the decline, the *New Yorker* made its appearance. Its founder, Harold Ross, was a most unlikely editor for a magazine which would soon be known for its suave and cosmopolitan tone. Born in Aspen, Colorado, Ross spent his early years as a reporter on the west coast. (Around the Press Club in San Francisco he was known as Roughhouse Ross.) During the war years, with the help of Alexander Woollcott and Franklin P. Adams, he made a great success of *Stars and Stripes,* the paper of the A.E.F. When he returned to America he met, through Woollcott, the members of the famous Algonquin (Hotel) Round Table and its auxiliary, the Thanatopsis Literary and Inside Straight Club. The doings and sayings of these wits – among them Woollcott, Heywood Broun, George S. Kaufman, Marc Connelly, and Dorothy Parker – were randomly reported in F. P. A.'s "The Conning Tower." Ross began to talk with these new friends about starting a humorous magazine. While he was for a short time a co-editor of *Judge,* he had shrewdly noted how far behind the times its humor was and how its editorial policies precluded improvement. Why should New York firms advertise in a magazine which was aimed at Dubuque, Iowa? He was certain there was an audience large enough in New York and other cities which looked to New York as *the* American metropolis to support the kind of magazine he intended to found.

About the only person who listened to Ross's scheme was his wife, Jane Grant. The Round Table set were mildly interested but all of them were well on the way in profitable careers of their own. (Seven of them did permit their names to be listed as "advisory editors" when the magazine appeared.) Fortunately Ross soon found a financial backer in Raoul Fleischmann, who cared little for the family baking business and who had money of his own to invest.

Ross's statement of purpose declared that the *New Yorker* would reflect metropolitan life. It would assume "a reasonable degree of enlightenment on the part of its readers" and they might expect a guide to what was going on in the arts, in sport and entertainment. There was no thought at the time that the *New Yorker* might one day be famous for its reportage and for such a totally unfunny piece as John Hersey's "Hiroshima" which filled the whole issue of August 31, 1946.

The year 1925 was a propitious moment to launch such a magazine as Ross dreamed of. Flourishing at the time were two magazines much nearer to the aims of the *New Yorker* than the older humor magazines – Condé Nast's *Vanity Fair* (1868–1936) and Mencken and Nathan's *Smart Set* (1890–1930). Their success indicated that new varieties of humorous writing were in demand. Most important in the success of Ross's venture was the fact that writers and cartoonists of the kind he sought were already at work and might be engaged, if he could pay enough. What was needed was a magnet to draw this abundant talent to one center.

Ross's flexibility was remarkable for a man with such strong convictions and prejudices. In the beginning he had no intention of publishing fiction. He was persuaded, and in time his magazine could be proud of having published stories by John O'Hara, Edward Newhouse, Jean Stafford, J. D. Salinger, Peter Taylor, and John Cheever. Ross was fondest of the "casuals" (short pieces of the kind *Punch* still favors) but some of his idea men sensed that the long piece was wanted, and so, beginning with the "profiles" (a distinctive *New Yorker* contribution), the long piece was in. The magazine moved with the times.

By the end of 1927 Ross had brought into the magazine the four assistants who would exert the greatest influence on its early shaping. Katharine Angell (later Mrs. E. B. White) joined the staff about six months after the first issue appeared. She was indispensable to Ross because of her sure taste and editorial acumen. White's first *New Yorker* piece so impressed her that she brought him to the attention of Ross who promptly gave him a job. The humanity of White's sketches, his Thoreauvian sensitivity to nature, and the uncluttered beauty of his prose balanced the brilliant cynicism of such writers as Dorothy Parker and Wolcott Gibbs. James Thurber, the third member of the group, came on the staff in 1927. Ross thought him a remarkable editor, which he was, though he repeatedly tried to shed the job. The fourth member, Wolcott Gibbs, also arrived in 1927. He was an able rewrite man and the magazine's most devastating parodist.

The anniversary number of February 23, 1929, shows that affluence had descended. The volume of advertising was already threatening the text. The formula and the format were set. This issue begins with "The Talk of the Town" and the first piece under it is "Notes and Comment," as it still is. There is a story by Dorothy Parker, one of James Thurber's "casuals" ("Our Own Modern English Usage"), a profile of Toscanini, a "Reporter at Large" piece by Alva Johnston. The hard-to-get Woollcott had been lured into the magazine to do his "Shouts and Murmurs" page. Genêt's "Paris Letter" is here. By this time, too, Ross could command the work of the cartoonists he admired. In this issue appear drawings by Peter Arno, Helen Hokinson (a discovery of which Ross was especially proud), Rea Irvin, Garrett Price, O. Soglow, Alan Dunn, and Mary Petty, Dunn's wife.

The *New Yorker*'s success caused a division in American humor. Since its editors aimed to attract sophisticated urban readers, they discarded the folksy humor which appeals in the dentist's office and the barbershop. It still circulates fitfully in some of the weekly magazines which continue to publish a page of cartoons and funny pieces.

In *A Subtreasury of American Humor* (1941) the E. B. Whites distribute their selections of modern sophisticated humor under thirteen categories. Four of these forms or varieties have been particular favorites in recent years: humorous verse; fables and other "moral" tales; burlesques and parodies; and nonsense.

Humorous or witty verse was, of course, no new thing in 1925. Freneau had used all the weapons of the satirist in his propaganda poems. Oliver Wendell Holmes' humorous poems, such as "The Deacon's Masterpiece" and "Cacoethes Scribendi," have lasted better than his patriotic and commemorative verse. The tradition continued in the poems of H. C. Bunner (editor of *Puck* from 1878 to 1896), Guy Wetmore Carryl, and Carolyn Wells. At the time the *New Yorker* was founded there were several masters of the mode: Arthur Guiterman; T. A. Daly, who made skilled use of the Italian-American dialect; Louis Untermeyer; and Samuel Hoffenstein (*Poems in Praise of Practically Nothing*, 1928). Some *New Yorker* favorites have been Guiterman, David McCord, Phyllis McGinley, Dorothy Parker, and Morris Bishop. Ogden Nash, a steady contributor for years, is said to have got the idea for his highly individual verse style from the formless country newspaper poems which F. P. A. occasionally copied into "The Conning Tower." His device of the long loping line which finally rimes continues to amuse, probably because there is so much witty social commentary between the rimes.

The humorous fable was no invention of the *New Yorker* wits, though they liked and developed the form. The "American Fables" of "M. Quad," already mentioned, are among the earliest adaptations of the genre in American writing. In Ambrose Bierce's *Collected Works* (Volume VI) there are four groups of fables: "Aesopus Emendatus," "Fables in Rhyme," "Fables from 'Fun'" (contributed to this English magazine in 1872–73), and "Fantastic Fables," which had been collected in book form in 1899. George Ade used the fable as an *embuscade* from which he could make quick sorties on culture-seekers and the newly rich. The letters of archy the cockroach to his boss, don marquis, often turn out to be fables, as in "warty bliggens the toad" and "aesop revised by archy."

Most of the recent fables border on fantasy or nonsense. James Thurber's *Fables for Our Time* (1940) and *Further Fables for Our Time* (1956) exhibit this variation especially well. It was inevitable that Thurber should become a fabulist. He drew animals incessantly, especially dogs. And what animals they are! – mixing imperturbably in the lives of the men and women whose business and pleasure they checkmate (the seal staring down from the headboard on the quarreling couple below; the rabbit behind the psychiatrist's desk). Many of Thurber's fables are of the classical Aesopian kind, with the improving moral stated at the end, such as that for "The Seal Who Became Famous," by leaving the seals and going out on the town (*Moral: Whom God has equipped with flippers should not monkey around with zippers*). But the best Thurber fables are the fantastic ones, like "The Owl Who Was God."

The humorous beast fable is as old as Aesop; parody begins with the pseudo-Homeric *Battle of the Frogs and the Mice.* Parody is closely related to travesty and burlesque, but it is the most sophisticated of these forms, concentrating on the style as well as the thought of the work which is being parodied. As Dwight Macdonald notes, in his *Parodies. An Anthology from Chaucer to Beerbohm – and After,* parody, at its best, is a form of literary criticism. It flourishes when there is a literate audience in the know to enjoy it. The parodist's prey is writing that irritates because it is too pretentious or too sentimental or too avant-garde.

There are many parodies in nineteenth-century American humor, though none of the professional humorists kept steadily at the trade, as Robert Benchley, Ring Lardner, Frank Sullivan, and Peter De Vries have done in our time. Poe was an excellent parodist and many of his early prose pieces are in this vein. Melville's *Pierre* opens with a subtle parody of romantic fiction, and later the account of the young Pierre's struggles to become a writer parodies the sentimental verse and prose of the mid-century. Parody turns up constantly in Mark Twain, from the burlesques written for the San Francisco weekly *The Golden Era* to the posthumously published "From an Unfinished Burlesque of Books on Etiquette" (*Letters from the Earth*, 1962). Bret Harte's *Condensed Novels* were so well liked that he put together a second collection.

But the great age of parody in America is the period from 1925 to the present. Apparently any writer of the *New Yorker* "school" could turn out good parodies. The listing of a few of the best will have to suffice: Ring Lardner's "Quadroon. A Play in Four Pelts Which May All Be Attended in One Day or Missed in a Group" (O'Neill's *Mourning Becomes Electra*); Benchley's "Shakespeare Explained. Carrying on the System of Footnotes to a Silly Extreme"; Frank Sullivan's "A Garland of Ibids" (Van Wyck Brooks's habit of rewriting his literary histories in page-usurping footnotes); E. B. White's "Across the Street and into the Grill" (Hemingway, of course) and his "Dusk in Fierce Pajamas" (a magazine dream after a surfeit of *Vogue* and *Harper's Bazaar*); Thurber's "*What* Cocktail Party?" (Martini-drenched chatter about T. S. Eliot's play); Wolcott Gibbs's "Death in the Rumble Seat (With the Usual Apologies to Ernest Hemingway)"; S. J. Perelman's "Waiting for Santy. A Christmas Playet (With a Bow to Mr. Clifford Odets)."

The high point in the parody renaissance may have been reached as early as 1929 when Harper's published Thurber and White's *Is Sex Necessary?* In the mid-twenties there was a spate of solemn books about sex and marriage, and the authors believed if things went on this way, the order of nature would be sadly changed. In their foreword they warn: "To prepare for marriage, young girls no longer assembled a hope chest – they read books on abnormal psychology. If they finally did marry, they found themselves with a large number of sex books on hand, but almost no pretty underwear. Most of them, luckily, never married at all – just continued to read." The sexologists had been home writing. "And meanwhile what was sex doing?" Thurber and White answer that question abundantly, though they never get round to the question in their title.

Nonsense humor is not gibberish. It leads somewhere though the reader is thrown for a loss if he tries to speculate where. As James Thurber remarked, it cannot be manufactured by writing opening sentences with nothing in mind, and then trying to create a story round them: such sentences as "Mrs. Ponsonby had never put the dog in the oven before" or "I have a wine tree, if you would care to see it." In the best nonsense humor the reader finds himself in a world where strange flowers with unbotanical names bloom menacingly, the slithy toves gyre and gimble in the wabe and the frumious Bandersnatch is to be shunned. The inhabitants of this nonsense world are sure of their sanity. Any outsider (like Alice) who questions their statements is rudely put in his place. Behind the seeming madness of this dream world of nonsense lurks a clue, just as the possible truth of a wild dream haunts us when we wake from it.

The Victorians were fond of nonsense humor, and with good reason, since they had Lewis Carroll and Edward Lear to provide it. Much nineteenth-century nonsense, American as well as English, borders on fantasy and whimsy in which there are satiric overtones. Modern nonsense humor of the *New Yorker* variety is wackier, zanier, more likely to shatter the nerves of the intruder who strays inside this world.

In his last years Ring Lardner wrote a series of short plays in this newer nonsense vein. They belong with the modern parodies but they also go over the line into dadaistic nonsense. One of the stage directions in "Clemo Uti – 'The Water Lilies' " will show the drift:

ACT IV: *A silo. Two Rats have got in there by mistake. One of them seems diseased. The other looks at him. They go out. Both Rats come in again and wait for a laugh. They don't get it, and go out. Wama enters from an off-stage barn. She is made up to represent the Homecoming of Casanova. She has a fainting spell. She goes out.*

James Thurber, the most versatile of modern humorists, seldom indulged in nonsense prose. He liked to let his verbal humor play close to the actual in order to burlesque the absurdities of American folkways. He limited his nonsense to his drawings in which strong-minded animals take over and reduce the humans who think they own the joint to imbecility. Frank Sullivan, mastermind of the Cliché Expert, generally takes off, as Thurber does, from some actual absurdity which catches his eye (lawyers' lingo, business English, family shows on the air) and shakes it, the way a dog shakes an old shirt. Occasionally Sullivan goes over the line into nonsense. By the time he has finished with the newspaper headline "Can Ban Gluts Beans Bins," the language has been shattered and Sullivan is "drunch punk – no – I am dunch prunk – no, no! – oh my God!"

Those who are old enough to have seen the Marx Brothers movies know what the nonsense humor of S. J. Perelman is like. Perelman was their gag writer and so perfect was the accommodation that it is hard to tell whether Perelman invented Groucho or Groucho thought up Perelman. The targets of Perelman's humor are advertising, Hollywood spectaculars, sentimental fiction, country living, the hard sell and the soft sell – in short, pretentious fraud wherever he finds it. Like Groucho, with his stern horn-rims, his leer, and his mobile eyebrows, Perelman insults you down, to make sure you damned well believe what he tells you. He gets along in this mad world by making people heel. His nonsense world is the world we live in, but without his self-appointed services we would be oblivious to the strange and often sinister goings-on.

Is the falling off in the volume of humor in the *New Yorker,* a fact which Ross and his editors were aware of and lamented as far back as 1938, an index to a general decline of American humorous writing? Certain kinds of American humor and the vehicles for conveying them have vanished. With a few exceptions the humorous newspaper column has gone. There are no more comic lecturers, though the extraordinary success of Hal Holbrook's imitation of Mark Twain as a platform comedian makes one wonder what would happen if a new Mark Twain offered himself to a booking agency. Comic writers who exploit their invented personalities, the Benchleys, Perelmans, Thurbers, have all but disappeared. Two possible routes along which such great comics as Bobby Clark, W. C. Fields, Bert Lahr, Jimmy Savo, the Marx Brothers, and Bob Hope traveled to stardom are gone: vaudeville and burlesque. In two media, however, the stage and the novel, there has been of late a notable increase in the volume of humorous writing.

As Broadway has ceased to risk serious and experimental plays, chiefly because of the great increase in production costs, the standard fare in the commercial theater has been reduced to two safe items: comedies and musicals. At the moment, also, Hollywood is betting on comedy to keep the movie industry going.

In the extraordinary group of novelists who made their start in the 1920's and 1930's there were few who had a bent for humor. One can find a comic scene here and there in the fiction of Dos Passos, Thomas Wolfe, and Hemingway. Though many of Fitzgerald's short stories, from which he principally made his living, are humorous or satiric, the themes of his novels are serious. The one novelist of this galaxy who moved with ease from tragedy to comedy was William Faulkner. He could also mingle the two, as he did in *As I Lay Dying*. When Faulkner finally got round to the invading Snopes family, in *The Hamlet* (1940), *The Town* (1957), and *The Mansion* (1959), he created a group of comic characters unequaled in American fiction.

Many of the novelists who emerged after World War II have turned away from serious themes or project them through wry or bitter comedy. What can one do or say, this turnabout seems to imply, in the face of world problems which statesmen blunder their way through while the threat of annihilation hovers over every decision taken? Better to cultivate your own garden and get some fun out of it if you can.

Taking their cue from Faulkner and – possibly – from some of the frontier humorists, many southern writers of fiction have exploited the possibilities for grotesque humor in the life of their region. As in the older southern humor, there is a battle going on between the ins and the outs, between respectability and instinctual, irrational behavior, country ways and city slickness. One finds many grotesque episodes in this fiction which, as Sut Lovingood remarked of his stories, may not "sit purfeckly quiet ontu the stumicks ove sum pussons" – as, for instance, the love affair between Faulkner's Ike Snopes and the cow and the hanging of the mule in Truman Capote's *Other Voices, Other Rooms*. There is also that pretty little love idyl, Flannery O'Connor's "Good Country People," about a sexually athletic Bible salesman and the female Ph.D. with a wooden leg. In Carson McCullers' *Ballad of the Sad Café* the final destructive fight between the ex-convict husband and the Amazonian wife is one of those community-shattering battles which southern humorists, old and new, have enjoyed writing about.

Among the talented writers of the newest generation are several novelists who have uncovered the vein of humor to be found in middle-class Jewish life. Saul Bellow, whose first two novels were bleak studies in despair and anxiety, produced in *The Adventures of Augie March* (1953) a modern picaresque novel whose hero, a young Jew on his way somewhere, falls into several hilarious predicaments. J. D. Salinger has made, by turns, tragedy, pathos, and comedy out of the intense relationships among the precocious children of his Glass family. The best stories in Bernard Malamud's *The Magic Barrel* (1958) deal with native Jewish material. In common with his second novel, *The Assistant* (1957), they offer insights into the suffering of Jews who live on the edge of poverty but who are saved from despair by their humor. Philip Roth's stories of Jewish middle-class life in *Goodbye, Columbus* (1959) are comedies of a high order. The funniest of them is "The Conversion of the Jews," in which young Ozzie Freeman backs Rabbi Binder into a corner over the argument whether God could have arranged matters so that Jesus could be born without intercourse.

When one stands back and looks at the condition of American humor at this moment, the most significant fact is its dispersal in the various mass media. Americans are listening to humor and looking at it more than they are reading it.

Of this humor produced in the mass media the "funnies" are the oldest. In the thousands of strip cartoons, adventure comics, horror comics which have come and gone since Outcault's "Yellow Kid" (1896), a few "comic comics" rose to a level which ensures them a place in any history of American humor: George Herriman's "Krazy Kat," Walt Kelly's "Pogo" (the college man's favorite), Milt Gross's "Nize Baby," and George Baker's indestructible "The Sad Sack."

Though the vaudeville comedians have vanished and the last of the comic lecturers was Will Rogers, comic entertainers of other kinds have taken their place. Sharp-tongued Mort Sahl delights the young with his anarchic comments on politics and business. Jonathan Winters is a one-man comedy in himself, since he is an excellent mimic and plays all the parts. Jewish vaudeville humor lives on in the song parodies of Allan Sherman, the darling of the Borscht circuit. Dick Gregory, the Negro entertainer, extracts laughter from serious matters. These performers have made their way from beatnik joints to black-tie nightclubs, and finally to a huge audience that hoards each new record they cut and follows them from one television show to another.

A still newer form of humorous entertainment is provided by such groups of young actors as the Second City performers in Chicago and New York. Taking their cue from a line of dialogue sent up from the audience, they will improvise a skit without going into a huddle. The masters of the improvised skit are Mike Nichols and Elaine May. Since their humor is their own invention and is the newest in form and the best we can hear and see (though not read) they deserve to be entered here as the latest arrivals among American humorists.

Selected Bibliography

History, Biography, and Criticism

Anderson, John Q., ed. *The Writings of Henry Clay Lewis* ("Madison Tensas, M.D."). Baton Rouge: Louisiana State University Press, 1962.

Becker, Stephen. *Comic Art in America.* New York: Simon and Schuster, 1959.

Benson, Ivan. *Mark Twain's Western Years.* Stanford, Calif.: Stanford University Press, 1938.

Blair, Walter. *Horse Sense in American Humor from Benjamin Franklin to Ogden Nash.* Chicago: University of Chicago Press, 1942. (See also Blair's *Native American Humor,* listed below, under Anthologies.)

——— and Franklin J. Meine, eds. *Half Horse Half Alligator: The Growth of the Mike Fink Legend.* Chicago: University of Chicago Press, 1956.

Boatright, Mody C. *Folk Laughter on the American Frontier.* New York: Macmillan, 1949. (Reprinted in paperback by Collier.)

Chittick, V. L. O. *Thomas Chandler Haliburton ("Sam Slick"): A Study in Provincial Toryism.* New York: Columbia University Press, 1924.

Dorson, Richard M. *American Folklore.* Chicago: University of Chicago Press, 1959.

Eastman, Max. *Enjoyment of Laughter.* New York: Simon and Schuster, 1936.

Ellis, Elmer. *Mr. Dooley's America: A Life of Finley Peter Dunne.* New York: Knopf, 1941.

Hoole, W. Stanley. *Alias Simon Suggs: The Life and Times of Johnson Jones Hooper.* University: University of Alabama Press, 1952.

Howe, Will D. "Early Humorists," in *The Cambridge History of American Literature,* Vol. II. New York: Macmillan, 1933. Pp. 148–59.

Hudson, Arthur Palmer. "Folklore," in *Literary History of the United States,* Vol. II. New York: Macmillan, 1948. Pp. 703–27.

Kramer, Dale. *Ross and the New Yorker.* Garden City, N.Y.: Doubleday, 1952.

Lynn, Kenneth S. *Mark Twain and Southwestern Humor.* Boston: Little, Brown, 1960.

Mott, Frank Luther. *A History of American Magazines,* Vols. II, III, and IV. Cambridge, Mass.: Harvard University Press, 1938, 1938, 1957. (For the humor magazines.)

Murrell, William. *A History of American Graphic Humor.* 2 vols.; New York: Whitney Museum of American Art, 1932.

Rickels, Milton. *Thomas Bangs Thorpe, Humorist of the Old Southwest*. Baton Rouge: Louisiana State University Press, 1962.

Rourke, Constance. *American Humor: A Study of the National Character*. New York: Harcourt, Brace, 1931.

Seitz, Don C. *Artemus Ward*. New York: Harper, 1919.

Shackford, James A. *David Crockett, the Man and the Legend*. Chapel Hill: University of North Carolina Press, 1956.

Stewart, George R. *John Phoenix, Esq., the Veritable Squibob: A Life of George H. Derby, U.S.A.* New York: Holt, 1937.

Tandy, Jennette. *Crackerbox Philosophers in American Humor and Satire*. New York: Columbia University Press, 1925.

Thompson, Harold W. *Body, Boots and Britches*. Philadelphia: Lippincott, 1940. (New York State folklore.)

———. "Humor," in *Literary History of the United States*, Vol. II. New York: Macmillan, 1948. Pp. 728–57.

Wade, John Donald. *Augustus Baldwin Longstreet*. New York: Macmillan, 1924.

Waugh, Coulton. *The Comics*. New York: Macmillan, 1947.

Whicher, George Frisbie. "Minor Humorists," in *The Cambridge History of American Literature*, Vol. III. New York: Macmillan, 1933. Pp. 21–30.

Wyman, Mary Alice. *Two American Pioneers, Seba Smith and Elizabeth Oakes Smith*. New York: Columbia University Press, 1927.

Yates, Norris W. *The American Humorist, Conscience of the Twentieth Century*. Ames: Iowa State University Press, 1964.

———. *William T. Porter and the Spirit of the Times: A Study of the Big Bear School of Humor*. Baton Rouge: Louisiana State University Press, 1957.

Anthologies

Blair, Walter. *Native American Humor (1800–1900)*. New York: American Book, 1937. (The basic work on American humor. It contains a 162-page historical introduction, an extensive bibliography, and a 350-page anthology of humorous writings. It was reissued in paperbound form in 1960 by the Chandler Publishing Company. In this edition the bibliography is reduced but it has been brought up to date and the introduction has been extended to cover twentieth-century developments.)

Botkin, B. A., ed. *A Treasury of American Folklore*. New York: Crown, 1944.

Carlisle, Henry C., Jr., ed. *American Satire in Prose and Verse*. New York: Random House, 1962.

Cerf, Bennett, ed. *An Encyclopedia of Modern American Humor*. Garden City, N.Y.: Doubleday, 1954.

Chittick, V. L. O., ed. *Ring-Tailed Roarers: Tall Tales of the American Frontier, 1830–1860*. Caldwell, Idaho: Caxton Printers, 1941.

Falk, Robert P., ed. *The Antic Muse: American Writers in Parody*. New York: Grove Press, 1956.

Hudson, Arthur Palmer, ed. *Humor of the Old Deep South*. New York: Macmillan, 1936.

Lynn, Kenneth S., ed. *The Comic Tradition in America*. Garden City, N.Y.: Doubleday, 1958.

Macdonald, Dwight, ed. *Parodies: An Anthology from Chaucer to Beerbohm — and After*. New York: Random House, 1960.

Mark Twain's Library of Humor. New York: Charles L. Webster, 1888.

Meine, Franklin J., ed. *Tall Tales of the Southwest*. New York: Knopf, 1930.

Simpson, Claude M., ed. *The Local Colorists: American Short Stories, 1857–1900*. New York: Harper, 1960.

Watterson, Henry, ed. *Oddities in Southern Life and Character*. Boston: Houghton Mifflin, 1882.

Weber, Brom, ed. *An Anthology of American Humor*. New York: Crowell, 1962.

Wells, Carolyn, ed. *Such Nonsense! An Anthology*. New York: Doran, 1918.

White, E. B., and Katharine S. White, eds. *A Subtreasury of American Humor*. New York: Modern Library (Random House), 1941.

Works by the Humorists

Whenever possible collected or selected works have been given, but in some instances it has been necessary to list a scarce first or early edition. Where paperbacks are available, the price is included.

Ade, George. *Fables in Slang and More Fables in Slang*. New York: Dover. $1.00.

Benchley, Robert. *The Benchley Roundup*. New York: Delta (Dell). $1.65.

Browne, Charles Farrar ("Artemus Ward"). *The Complete Works of Artemus Ward*. New York: G. W. Dillingham, 1898.

Clemens, Samuel L. ("Mark Twain"). *The Washoe Giant in San Francisco*, edited by Franklin Walker. San Francisco: George Fields, 1938. (Sketches printed in the *Golden Era*.)

Crockett, David. *The Autobiography of David Crockett*. New York: Scribner's, 1923. (Also prints two other — spurious — accounts of Crockett's exploits.)

Derby, George Horatio ("Phoenix"). *Phoenixiana*. New York: Appleton, 1856.

———. ("Squibob") *The Squibob Papers*. New York: Carleton, 1865.

Dunne, Finley Peter ("Mister Dooley"). *Mr. Dooley at His Best*, edited by Elmer Ellis. New York: Scribner's, 1938.

Haliburton, Thomas Chandler. *The Clockmaker: First, Second and Third Series*. New York: George Monro, 1880.

Harris, George Washington. *Sut Lovingood's Yarns.* New York: Dick and Fitzgerald, 1867.

Harris, Joel Chandler. *The Complete Tales of Uncle Remus,* compiled by Richard Chase. Boston: Houghton Mifflin, 1955.

Hooper, Johnson Jones. *Simon Suggs' Adventures and Travels . . . with Widow Rugby's Husband, and Twenty-Six Other Humorous Tales of Alabama.* Philadelphia: T. B. Peterson, 1856.

Lardner, Ring. *The Ring Lardner Reader,* edited by Maxwell Geismar. New York: Scribner's, 1963.

Locke, David Ross ("Petroleum V. Nasby"). *The Nasby Papers.* Indianapolis: C. O. Perrine, 1864.

———. *The Struggles of Petroleum V. Nasby.* Boston: Beacon. $2.45.

Longstreet, Augustus Baldwin. *Georgia Scenes.* New York: American Century (Hill and Wang). $1.25.

Marquis, Don. *archy and mehitabel.* New York: Dolphin (Doubleday). $.95.

———. *The Best of Don Marquis,* edited by Christopher Morley. Garden City, N.Y.: Doubleday, 1946.

Newell, Robert Henry. ("Orpheus C. Kerr"). *The Orpheus C. Kerr Papers.* First, second, and third series. 3 vols.; New York: Carleton, 1865.

Perelman, S. J. *The Most of S. J. Perelman.* New York: Simon and Schuster. $2.45.

Shaw, Henry Wheeler ("Josh Billings"). *Everybody's Friend, or Josh Billings' Encyclopedia and Proverbial Philosophy of Wit and Humor.* Hartford, Conn.: American Publishing Company, 1874.

Smith, Seba. *My Thirty Years out of the Senate, by Major Jack Downing.* New York: Oaksmith, 1859. (Contains both series of Downing letters.)

Sullivan, Frank. *A Pearl in Every Oyster.* New York: Universal Library (Grosset and Dunlap). $1.65.

———. *A Rock in Every Snowball.* New York: Universal Library. $1.45.

Thompson, William Tappan. *Major Jones's Courtship.* Philadelphia: Carey, 1844.

———. *Major Jones's Chronicles of Pineville.* Philadelphia: Carey and Hart, 1845.

Thorpe, Thomas Bangs. *The Mysteries of the Backwoods.* Philadelphia: Carey and Hart, 1846.

———. *The Hive of "The Bee-Hunter."* New York: Appleton, 1854.

Thurber, James. *The Owl in the Attic.* New York: Universal Library. $1.25.

———. *The Thurber Carnival.* New York: Dell. $.75.

———. *Thurber Country.* New York: Simon and Schuster. $1.45.

White, E. B. *One Man's Meat.* New York: Torchbooks (Harper and Row). $1.85.

———. *Quo Vadimus?* New York: Universal Library. $1.25.

literature

UNIVERSITY OF MINNESOTA PAMPHLETS ON AMERICAN WRITERS

William Van O'Connor, Allen Tate, Leonard Unger, and Robert Penn Warren, editors

Willard Thorp, Karl Shapiro, and Philip Rahv, advisers

1. ERNEST HEMINGWAY — by Philip Young
2. ROBERT FROST — by Lawrance Thompson
3. WILLIAM FAULKNER — by William Van O'Connor
4. HENRY JAMES — by Leon Edel
5. MARK TWAIN — by Lewis Leary
6. THOMAS WOLFE — by C. Hugh Holman
7. RECENT AMERICAN DRAMA — by Alan S. Downer
8. T. S. ELIOT — by Leonard Unger
9. WALT WHITMAN — by Richard Chase
10. GERTRUDE STEIN — by Frederick J. Hoffman
11. WALLACE STEVENS — by William Y. Tindall
12. EDITH WHARTON — by Louis Auchincloss
13. HERMAN MELVILLE — by Leon Howard
14. THE AMERICAN SHORT STORY — by Danforth Ross
15. F. SCOTT FITZGERALD — by Charles E. Shain
16. RECENT AMERICAN POETRY — by Glauco Cambon
17. EDWIN ARLINGTON ROBINSON — by Louis Coxe
18. JOHN CROWE RANSOM — by John L. Stewart
19. BENJAMIN FRANKLIN — by Theodore Hornberger
20. JOHN DOS PASSOS — by Robert Gorham Davis
21. NATHANAEL WEST — by Stanley Edgar Hyman
22. RECENT AMERICAN NOVELISTS — by Jack Ludwig
23. NATHANIEL HAWTHORNE — by Hyatt H. Waggoner
24. WILLIAM CARLOS WILLIAMS — by John Malcolm Brinnin
25. WASHINGTON IRVING — by Lewis Leary
26. EZRA POUND — by William Van O'Connor
27. SINCLAIR LEWIS — by Mark Schorer
28. KATHERINE ANNE PORTER — by Ray B. West, Jr.
29. JAMES T. FARRELL — by Edgar M. Branch
30. THEODORE ROETHKE — by Ralph J. Mills, Jr.
31. REINHOLD NIEBUHR — by Nathan A. Scott, Jr.
32. LITTLE MAGAZINES — by Reed Whittemore
33. ELLEN GLASGOW — by Louis Auchincloss
34. THORNTON WILDER — by Bernard Grebanier
35. HENRY WADSWORTH LONGFELLOW — by Edward Hirsh
36. WILLA CATHER — by Dorothy Van Ghent
37. AMBROSE BIERCE — by Robert A. Wiggins
38. CONRAD AIKEN — by Reuel Denney
39. ALLEN TATE — by George Hemphill
40. ARTHUR MILLER — by Robert Hogan
41. RALPH WALDO EMERSON — by Josephine Miles
42. AMERICAN HUMORISTS — by Willard Thorp
43. SHERWOOD ANDERSON — by Brom Weber
44. ROBERT PENN WARREN — by Paul West

EACH PAMPHLET, 65 CENTS

UNIVERSITY OF MINNESOTA PRESS, Minneapolis, Minnesota 55455, U.S.A.
Distributed to high schools in the United States by Webster Division
McGRAW-HILL BOOK COMPANY
St. Louis New York San Francisco Dallas